The Second Income

Acknowledgements

I would like to thank the people who have bought this book, because they've decided to put themselves in the focus to achieve an even better quality of life.

My appreciation goes to all the business people who offered me good insights behind the scenes of the 'Second Income'.
Thank you, also for the positive references and the requests for expansions that I realized with this version of the book that has been extended by several chapters.

Furthermore I would like to extend my most special thanks to Petra Grundke and Kevin Reuther for their excellent cooperation and also to my wife Evelyn to whom I dedicate this book.

Eike Clausius

The Second Income

Eike Clausius

1st Edition

Berlin 2016

Bibliographical data of the Deutsche Nationalbibliothek (German National Library):
The Deutsche Nationalbibliothek lists this publication in the Deutsche Nationalbibliografie; detailed bibliographic information is available on the Internet via http://dnb.dnb.de.

© 2016 Dr. Eike Clausius

Illustration: Dr. Clausius Consulting / Kevin Reuther
Translation: Dr. Clausius / Kevin Reuther

Produced and published by: BoD – Books on Demand, Norderstedt

ISBN: 9-7837-3921-188-6

Table of Contents

5

Introduction

During the last decades a lot of things have changed in terms of economics – especially in technologically highly advanced countries such as the USA, Japan and the European countries including Germany. The employment situation will adapt to the ongoing globalisation and dynamic markets. Looking for a permanent employer as it was taught to our children does not work anymore today. The working environment has fundamentally changed.

Maybe you have already experienced that you work and work, but thereby feel controlled and steered. As an employee, you realise that your lifetime is determined by your company's work cycle, and that you **exchange lifetime for money**. As an entrepreneur – especially in small and medium sized businesses – you might also get the feeling of being other-directed, for example by your responsibility towards your employees and their individual health and life situation. You invest all of your lifetime in your business and realise that there is less and less time for family, friends and for yourself?

"If your business depends on you,
you don't own a business – you have a job.
And it's the worst job in the world
because you're working for a lunatic!"
Michael E. Gerber

In this case, the 'madness' is about someone who believed in something that was not real. A real entrepreneur is free. He takes responsibility, but his business is not depending on him. He rather works on his company than for his company. Especially the often-described 'freelancers' who are free to work all the time, cannot escape the so-called trap of the '**rat race**'. Their lives are often determined by their work. You might sometimes get the feeling that this thing you suspect to be the 'career ladder' is nothing more than this '**rat race**' from the inside. Would you be interested in a chance to improve that situation? The following is intended to describe a method to help you do so.

Let us take a look at the possibilities of improving the above-described situation. Imagine you could get to know something where you…

1. don't need any capital investment,

2. can freely choose your workplace,

3. are in the centre of your life,

4. can become independent – step by step,

5. get paid adequately,

6. can build up a global team,

7. can achieve an inheritable financial income,

8. can build up a pension – independent from the statutory pension payments and without any payments.

Some might already know this concept, because it developed from the **word-of-mouth-recommendation**: You recommend a good movie or a good book, or you talk to someone about the quality of your car.

Also in the 'ordinary economy', some companies know that product recommendations might be rewarded with a onetime commission. Usually, these are financial or material bonuses, such as coffee makers or tools. But how many of those machines do you need? Besides, you are not involved in any follow-up business.

In the course of this publication, some of the following aspects will be mentioned:

1. How does such marketing of recommendations work?

2. How can recommendations be classified concerning the different distribution channels?

3. How can Referral Marketing be described in terms of its structure and financial aspects?

4. *What are the perspectives of achieving a 'SECOND INCOME'
   with this kind of marketing?*

5. *Which personal freedom could you achieve – for you and for
   others – to live a self-determined life?*

This book shall come up with an answer to these and many other
questions.

Notes

Presentation of distribution channels

Overview

The following figure underlines which classifications of distribution channels exist related to building a marketing concept based on recommendations (the **concept of Referral Marketing**).

Classification of distribution channels
related to Referral Marketing

Relevant distribution channels are introduced and could be considered as a path towards Referral Marketing. However, other distribution channels as for example wholesale are neglected due to their minor relevance. Retail therefore presents the first distribution channel and can be subdivided into traditional retail and direct sales. According to this structure, a development towards Referral Marketing through direct sales and Network Marketing can be seen. Furthermore, franchising should be introduced as a further distribution channel that can be put into the context of this development. It combines aspects of (distribution-)networks with traditional retail.

Traditional retail

In the traditional or classic retail sector goods are moved from a **wholesaler** via an **intermediary** and a **retaile**r to the customer. The wholesalers often are either companies operating abroad and importing goods, or exporters who distribute goods. Intermediaries are usually located nationally and distribute goods to the retailers. The **gross price** – the price that is paid by the customer – is the **net price** increased by the VAT rate. This issue is introduced by the following figure 'Structure of a customer price - retail'. The customer needs to pay for the production as well as for each distributor. This means that approximately 70% of the final price is determined by the distribution from wholesaler to intermediary and retailer!

The composition of a customer price – retail

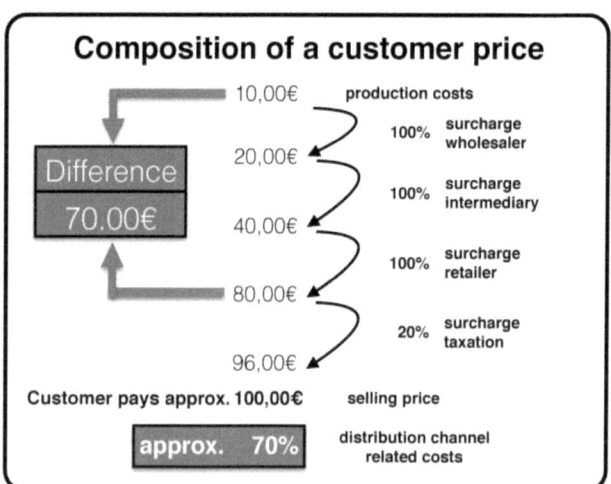

Usually, the retailers have the highest risk. They need to pre-finance goods, pay rent for the stores, and additionally need to pay for things like gas, water, heating, salaries of employees, insurance and a huge number of social contributions. Thus, a lot of **(life-)time** is needed to plan all these activities properly.

Many retailers can surely understand this situation, because they often are under budgetary and/or time pressure. However, such investments might pay off and lead to a certain financial inde-pendence under the right circumstances.

In the franchise sector the producer or franchisor decides to market his goods (or services) with a properly tested business model. This can be described as system business or system gastronomy. The brand and the business concept are well known, but the 'freelancer' is bound by the instructions and the concept of the franchisor and therefore has no freedom of choice concerning the marketing of his goods.

The entrepreneur or franchisee has the opportunity to make decisions concerning human resources, regional advertisements, or renting property. Besides that, he is bound by the requirements of the franchise system. Any changes or new concepts need to be approved by the franchisor. The reliability of an existing and well operating concept, however, limits the freedom to take entrepreneurial decisions. The strength of this distribution channel is that goods of equal quality are presented in an equal way on the world market.

Franchisees pay a one-time **entry fee**, which can be an up to 7-digit Euro amount. This includes the business concept, all additional services of the franchisor including brand utilisation (Clausius & Schütz, 2014), product- and system-know-how as well as marketing. Furthermore, there usually is a revenue share of the franchisor.

Direct sales means that the producer decides to market his goods with sales partners (distributors). At the distribution channel of **traditional direct sales**, independent distributors (also called advisors) buy the producer's goods to resell them to the customers who need to pay the gross price.

Usually, this business is about durable consumer goods requiring explanations (Clausius, 2014, S. 19) that can be used over several years such as industrial machines, cars or cameras. The producer delivers the goods to his trusted sales partners. They usually experience a local, regional or country specific territorial protection.

The composition of a customer price – direct sales

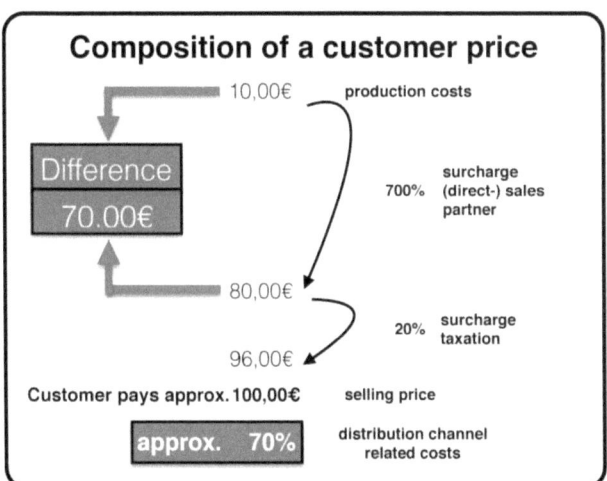

The creation of a sales or distribution structure is allowed or even desired. This means that a sales partner can work independently or even have his own employees who support him with the advisory and sales processes. The sales partner usually buys goods with 30-50% discount directly from the producer and resells them to the customers with an appropriate surcharge. He needs to be a real expert for all the producer's goods to be able to advise the customers properly.

In the case of **durable consumer goods** like vacuum cleaners, he will usually do that once and the product can be used for several years. In the case of **non-durable consumer goods** like, for example, the equivalent vacuum cleaner bags customers usually need to be motivated on a regular basis to purchase the original products (Clausius, 2014, S. 19). New customers need to be acquired frequently, whereby the time factor can become a huge barrier. Therefore, in the traditional retail as well as the direct sales business, (life-)time is exchanged for money.

The majority of the sales price remains with the advisor, who however, has to pay his employees' fixed salaries and/or bonuses. In this business, high sales prices can lead to high commissions and therefore high incomes.

Traditional Network Marketing is a certain kind of **direct sales** where goods are delivered directly from the producer to the customer using sales partners. Legally, sales partners buy goods from the producer, but they are delivered directly from the producer to the customer. It makes sense to market either low-priced durable consumer goods requiring explanations, or non-durable consumer goods that do not require frequent promotion through the sales partner. The creation of a sales structure is allowed and expected, because durable consumer goods especially need frequent acquisition due to their long lifecycle, which means that new customers need to be found frequently, because durable consumer goods are used over long periods of time (Clausius, 2014, S. 19).

Network Marketing includes sales as well as the mediation of goods through sales partners directly to the final consumer. Furthermore, the possibility to create your own sales structure is provided (Zacharias, Michael (Bundesverband, 2005)).

Referral Marketing is using a business
to support humans,
while other branches are using humans
to support businesses
according to Rich de Vos

Referral Marketing is completely different from traditional direct sales and Network Marketing, especially because most of us have already used this kind of marketing, but without receiving any reward. If you, for example, go on an enjoyable trip with a good tour operator, it is "the most natural thing in the world" (Steiner, 2014, S. 56) to recommend him or her. You might tell your friends about your experiences – without any background knowledge or 'need to practise'. You talk about it because it was inspiring. This word of mouth is Referral Marketing. You share a positive experience with a friend or an acquaintance and that makes you absolutely credible.

In his book "The Business of the 21st Century" (Kiyosaki, Fleming, & Kiyosaki, The Business of the 21st Century, 2012), **Robert T. Kiyosaki** comes up with eight reasons why Network Marketing as Referral Marketing makes people's life more fulfilled and their future safer:

1. *functional business education,*
2. *profitable way to economic growth,*
3. *friends with equal values and dreams,*
4. *the power of owning your network,*
5. *a duplicatable, fully scalable business,*
6. *amazing leadership,*
7. *a mechanism to create real wealth,*
8. *big dreams and the power to live them.*

Referral Marketing is different from Network Marketing, because recommendation-makers get their commissions for recommending goods only from the producer.

Every Referral Marketing is a Network-Marketing
but not every Network-Marketing is a Referral Marketing.
Eike Clausius

A sale does not take place, and also makes no sense, because every product user pays the same purchase price. In legal terms, therefore, the recommendation-makers do not sell any goods to the customers. Successful people in the Referral Marketing business are not characterised by their good selling abilities, but by their systematic approach and a high percentage of emotional intelligence (Clausius, 2015). Referral Marketing makes sense especially for **non-durable consumer good**s.

Distribution channels in qualitative comparison

Criteria-related comparison of distribution channels

In this part, the presented distribution channels – retail, franchise, Network Marketing and Referral Marketing – will be compared and contrasted in consideration of different criteria.

The following table shows qualitative criteria as well as various advantages and disadvantages of the different distribution channels. Some of those criteria will be explained in an exemplary fashion below.

Firstly we will consider **license fees**. As a franchisee you usually pay a relatively high sum of licence fees – either once or regularly at pre-defined dates. In exchange, you receive certain services. As a retailer, you also need to develop your own marketing concept, but you do not pay any license fees. You invest in a certain concept on your own. You are self-employed. This self-employment applies also to those who are in the Network Marketing business. They usually have relatively low license fees that include using the existing marketing concept. In the case of Referral Marketing there are no license fees to be paid and the given concepts - a **complete implementation plan** - may be used for free.

A further very important distinguishing criterion is the **location**. While you are geographically bound in the cases of franchising and retail, Network Marketing and Referral Marketing offer you the opportunity to work worldwide.

Comparison of franchise – retail
– Network Marketing and Referral Marketing
(according to (Ihringer, 2014))[1;2;3]

Description	Retail	Franchise	Network Marketing	Referral Marketing
License fees	no	high	niedrig	no
Store fittings	high	high	niedrig	no
geographically bound	yes	yes	no	no
Fixed costs	high	high	depending on products	no
Employees	possible	yes	no	no
Bank loan necessary	possible	yes	possible	no
work experience necessary	yes	yes	no	no
Limited income	yes/ depending on structure	yes	yes/ limited levels	no
Marketing plan focused on	product turnover	product turnover	selling	recommen- dation
Existence of subscription systems	no	no	yes	yes
Trade margin	yes	yes	possible	no
Return on sales	low	low	medium	high
Education/ training	cost-intensive	cost-intensive	low	low/free
Club	Sales-Club/ structured sales	Franchise- Club	Sales-Club	Consumer- Club
Realisation plan	individual	complete implementation plan	complete implementation plan	complete implementation plan
Focus on	business	business	business/ people	people
Owned by	shareholders/ private possession	shareholders	shareholders/ private possession	private possession
Delivery of goods by	store/ producer	store	producer	producer

Some major differences regarding the distribution channels are also given concerning the **employees**: In the case of a franchise concept it is a frequent practice and mostly necessary to have several employees. As already mentioned, this leaves you in the difficult position of being dependent on their individual health

---

[1] **Sales-Clubs** are associations of distributors and their partners.
[2] **Franchise-Clubs** are associations of franchisors and franchisees to estab- lish a good communication between those parties.
[3] **Consumer-Clubs** are associations of suppliers and demanders to ensure proper advisory, common discounts as well as other services.

and personal situation. In the retail sector, it depends on the size and type of your business how many employees you might need. If the size requires several employees, you are in the same position as the franchisee. If you work alone, you face another challenge: If you are going on holiday, your income does the same. And whenever you fall ill, your income 'is going on holiday', too. You do not earn anything during those times. In the case of Network Marketing and Referral Marketing, you usually have no employees. Especially as a referral marketer, your personal situation is relieved, because money flows constantly when you build your network systemically. This will be explained in detail in the following chapters.

We will now look at the criterion of the **limit for the income**. Your income is limited in the case of franchising, because there are certain opening hours, working hours and a certain size of the business. In the retail sector and the network-marketing business, you have a limited income as well. The retail business is based on a structure that can vary from only one single store up to a chain of stores. From a certain number of employees onwards one might not be able to lead this business alone anymore. Another barrier can be found in the case of Network Marketing. This barrier appears because of the compensation plans, which are cancelled at a defined level where no commissions are paid anymore. Only Referral Marketing has none of those barriers.

Trade margins generally describe a (percentage) surcharge on a product price before the product is resold. Such surcharges can be found in the franchising as well as the retail business. In the case of Network Marketing these surcharges are possible, but the individual decision rests with the company. In the case of Referral Marketing, however, all products are offered on the market for the same price. The referrer does not sell anything.

By looking into **training measures** one can easily see the huge advantages of Referral Marketing compared to the other distribution channels. The costs of such events or material that might be provided online do not need to be paid by the referrer. Network Marketing businesses offer a huge number of training measures as well, but they usually want you to participate in the costs. In the franchise and retail business, you generally have to pay the costs of such measures on your own.

One last interesting aspect that should be highlighted is about the **relation of person and business**. While most companies (in retail, franchise and Network Marketing) put their main focus on the business, Referral Marketing is seeking new ways. At this point, a quote of Rich de Vos should be highlighted: Referral Marketing is using a business to support humans, while other branches are using humans to support businesses. What does that mean? The focus is on the people.

It is rather obvious that people are required for a well operating business in retail and franchise. In the Referral Marketing business, those people are supported. The process of increasing systematisation and professionalisation of your recommendations supports your personal development. This is an ongoing process that, for example, has an impact on your communicative and entrepreneurial skills. You therefore also support others by teaching them in the Referral Marketing business, giving them the opportunity to develop the same skills: On the one hand, you recommend a product that you appreciate. On the other hand, you offer a possibility to try Referral Marketing and to experience personal development and improvement. This also highlights the huge importance of being keen to learn something new.

Notes

This section will present some criteria for the distinction between employees, entrepreneurs and referral marketers.

Comparison of employees – entrepreneurs – referral marketers
(according to (Ihringer, 2014))

Criteria	Employee	Entrepreneur	Referral Marketer
Working time	38 to 40-hour week	50 to 80-hour week	10 to 40-hour week
Vacation	25 – 30 / contractually regulated	often hard to plan	freedom of choice
Business situation	dependency and often low motivation	independency, but often lots of stress and difficult economic situation, also often left to their own	wide degree of independency and free allocation of time, mentors/contact persons, are available to help and support if desired
Income (monthly)	400 € – 6.000 €	1.000 € – 20.000 € plus	300 € – 30.000 € plus

Considering the aspect of **working hours**, one can already identify huge differences. As an employee, you have the 'usual 40-hours week' with little or even no flexibility at all.

As an entrepreneur, you have a weekly workload that might be much higher than 40 hours, especially during the founding period of your business. And you get even less if you relate it to your expenditure of time. In the case of Referral Marketing, however, the expenditure of time is directly proportional to the financial success. You can moreover get the support of people who 'know how the wind blows' – **mentors**.

The table clarifies that a significantly lower expenditure of time is generally needed in Referral Marketing. This is understandable when you reconsider the previously presented criteria like a well-working and well-tested existence or the possibility to use a **complete implementation plan** with an existing marketing concept.

This flexibility can also be found in your **vacation options**. While an employee has fixed vacation times, entrepreneurs and referral marketers can decide on their own when and how much vacation they want. However, as a referral marketer, you get your monthly commission – your 'SECOND INCOME' – which is usually not the case for entrepreneurs.

A very interesting aspect arises when we compare the respective individual **operational situations** of employees with that of employers. A Gallup Study from 2014 indicates that on average 70 percent of the **employees** have an 'unengaged attitude towards their employer or company'. As much as 15 percent have already made their minds up to hand in their resignation at some point in the future. (Gallup GmbH & Financial Times Deutschland, 2014) In other words, one could state that around 80 percent of employees do not enjoy what they are doing anymore. Many of them think about alternatives.

Entrepreneurs often suffer from stress and pressure at work. They face bureaucratic barriers each day, a huge tax burden, and a bad or moody economic environment. Political stability is often missing and the banks complicate investments.

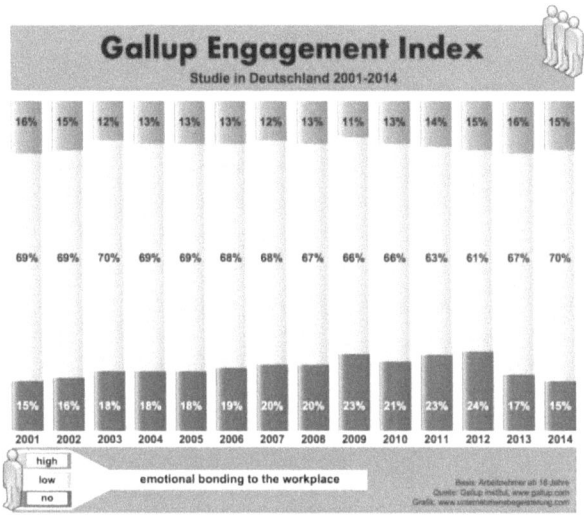

In **Referral Marketing** on the other hand, you benefit from the possibilities of flexible time management and the already mentioned free choice of workplace. One can do this job full-time as well as part-time. You are able to create your own working environment where communicating with other people plays a central role. You can choose what kind of people you intend to contact and cooperate with. In Referral Marketing, you create your very own working environment with the people you want to get involved with! Traditional office tasks such as writing bills, accounting, warehousing, or workforce planning can almost be dropped completely, because the Referral Marketing company is taking care of them.

27

Lastly, the **monthly income** should be analysed and compared. As an average worker, you might be familiar with the problem of having no more than 500€[4] to spend for things other than rent and other fixed overheads. Sometimes it might even be hard to make ends meet.

Small entrepreneurs often have the problem of earning much less than **employees** receive as a **salary**. They face the already mentioned burdens of self-employment such as long working-hours, very limited holidays and stress.

An average entrepreneur can surely make between 5.000€ and 15.000€ a month, but only a few top-earners earn more than 20.000€ per month. In contrast to the **employees' income**s, these, however, are gross-incomes where social contributions and other duties will be deducted.

The average **part-time worker in Referral Marketing** earns between 300€ and 1.500€ a month. **Full-time workers in Referral Marketing** might earn – related to the individual time spent – between 5.000€ and 25.000€. **Experts** who are working consistently with the **Referral Marketing** concepts might even earn considerably more than 30.000€.

---

[4] In the whole book the German numerical system is used. That means one thousand Euros and zero cent is written as follows: 1.000,00 €.

First, I'd like to share a little story with you. All the time, there are people who dream of being self-employed – of becoming an entrepreneur. This dream is about self-fulfilment as Maslow describes it, and the related opportunity for greater freedom. Sadly, most of them end up with 'being free to work' all the time, and they lose all their freedom.

In contrast, we can see that employees have 2 days off every week plus the public holidays. That adds up to 115 to 120 free days per year – without considering the number of vacation days. Employees can therefore roughly calculate on 150 days off per year.

"And you became self-employed?" Do you really have more freedom, more autonomy, self-fulfilment and wealth?

If we take **true wealth** to be the freedom and the ability to live your own life with all your personal dreams and wishes, we must raise the question of how this can be realised.

So, what is keeping you from being successfully self-employed in the Referral Marketing business?

People are characterised by their personal environment. Maybe your parents have been working for someone and you want to do the same now. You want to follow the example of your parents. But if you want to decide about your future life on your own, you may open your mind for new developments and leave the old paths behind. You make the decisions about your life.

The challenges of our time such as unemployment, the bank crisis, or pollution will not be solved by those who have created them. Only if people are willing and ready to take responsibility for the future generations, things might change (Clausius, 2012).

The same is true for radically new business models and the responsibility towards your business partners.

Let us assume that there is only one barrier between you and the possibility of being self-employed: **Fear**.

It might be the fear of starting a business on your own, without someone at your side. You might fear the incalculable risk and the huge amount of time and money needed. You might also fear losing your 'safe employment situation' and that you would need to work sixty or eighty hours per week. You would give up what you have done before, what you experienced as 'security'. You might also believe that you have a huge lack of experience in founding a company, and a lack of knowledge in economics as well. Maybe you think that you need to attend a **start-up seminar**, because you also have no knowledge about business financing (Clausius, 1999) or accounting (Clausius, 1998). And you might worry about being alone and having no support of a partner or mentor.

In the Referral Marketing business, you do not need to worry about any of those issues: You can start from the 'safe basis' of your existing employment and you don't need to invest any money. At the beginning, the only thing you need is a few hours per week. If it does not work for you, you still have the alleged security of your current workplace. If you need or want it, you also have the opportunity of permanent support through mentors.

If you want to convince yourself of the quality of your Referral Marketing company's goods first, you should definitely use them on your own. Related to that, you should also consider that the owner of a restaurant does not start a business to eat a lot of food, but to establish a successful business. He does not need to be his own best customer. You can trust and build on the experiences of others. With a good mixture of your own experiences and some references, you can leave any insecurity behind.

Notes

In the Referral Marketing business, it rarely happens that someone is successful immediately. It is about building up success over the long term.

It is possible to establish an income with a simple and systematic approach within three or four years that is equal to an income in the 'ordinary business world', which is usually worth 30 or 40 years.

Currently, most people 'graft' 30 or 40 years for one employer to finally enjoy some 'big travelling' at their retirement age. According to recent German law, however, this means that you are supposed to finance your travels with less than 50% of your last net salary. In other words, there will be a lack of time, and – in the worst case – a lack of money. Referral Marketing could enable you to realise your dreams much quicker. The sustained success in Referral Marketing is build upon continuous and systematic activities, which are successful when 'implemented in a proper way'.

If someone is talking about '**fast success**' in this business, this usually happens because of specific circumstances. People who reach the top leadership positions in Referral Marketing usually have a specific background. Some of the reasons why those people build a huge network within just one month could be:

1. *The person was principal for more than 30 years. He also gave sport lessons. Everyone knew him and everyone trusted him. In short: Almost every resident went to his school. How could you decline an offer of someone who was your lecturer and educator?*

2. *The person went from door to door and everyone he talked to became a business partner. The person's father was a member of the city council and owned many of the houses around. So,*

the residents thought it would be the best to simply do what he was suggesting.

3. The person has already had 20 years of experience in the Referral Marketing business. He has a huge number of contacts, relationships and friends – people who knew, respected and trusted him. Because this person was already very successful with another business, he was able to establish a huge new network very fast. This person has somehow prepared this 'instant success' for the last 20 years.

'**Instant success**' in the Referral Marketing business is rather rare. This business is not about fast results, but about growing results – about 'd o i n g' something. You should deserve your success and it can therefore be said:

„We serve before we deserve"
according to Henry Ford

This is also the reason why some people develop faster than others in the Referral Marketing business. If you are in a situation where you rarely have any connections to other people, the concept of Referral Marketing enables you to build some new relationships. After that, your personal network starts to grow. This enables your business to grow as well – through further recommendations!

Distribution channels in quantitative comparison

The potential of duplication

When people think about growth, they are used to thinking about linear and steady growth. But let us have a look at the meaning of exponential growth. Some might be familiar with the 'chess board-rice grain-example'[5], but only few people know about its practical relevance.

To establish a 'SECOND INCOME' with Referral Marketing you *n e e d* to explain to your partners that it is very important to focus on serious candidates rather than to try and recommend something to the whole world.

One can distinguish different kinds of duplication in the Referral Marketing business. If the marketing concept is reproduced once per month, this is called **Single-Duplication** (**1-Duplication**). It can also be reproduced twice, which is called **Double-Duplication** (**2-Duplication**), or even five times, which is called **Fiver-Duplication** (**5-Duplication**).

_____

[5] The inventor of the **chess game** impressed his king so much that this king granted him a wish. He 'only' wished for the **chessboard** to be filled **with rice grains**. One grain one the first field, two grains on the second field, and four on the third field and so on. So the rice grains were doubled on each field to come. The king thought that this modest wish should surely be fulfilled. If he had known something about maths, he surely would not have agreed. On the 64th field of the chessboard would have been 9.223.372.036.854.775.808 rice grains. With the sum of 18.446.744.073.709.600.000 rice grains you would be able to cover the whole planet earth.

Please bear in mind what it could mean if you recommend your concept to **o n e   s i n g l e   person** per month only, and help him or her develop their business.

Numerical series of the 1-Duplication

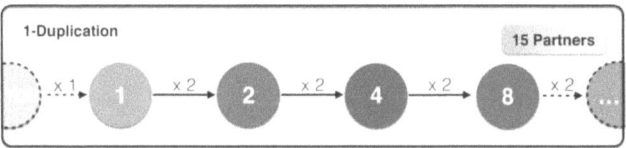

You can furthermore show the difference to the **Double-Duplication** by introducing the following numerical series: (Failla, 2002, S. 13ff.), (Failla, 2008, S. 19ff.)

Numerical series of the 2-Duplication

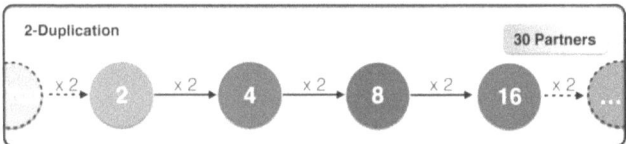

This numerical series[6] presents the potentiation of your Referral Marketing business if you and each of your partners introduce **t w o 'serious partners'** to your business per month. You recommend your business to **only   o n e   more person** per month. If you pass on this approach continuously, you will have 30 new partners in your team within just four months. The size of your **team** has **doubled**!

---

[6] Note: If your opponent is not able to understand this relatively simple piece of maths, stop calculating anything else for this person. You would get yourself into trouble.

What would the numerical series look like if you and your team reached **t h r e e** **'serious partners'** every month? You explain to those 'reliable guys', how they could support three people as well. This makes nine '**new** partners' for you.

Numerical series of the 3-Duplication

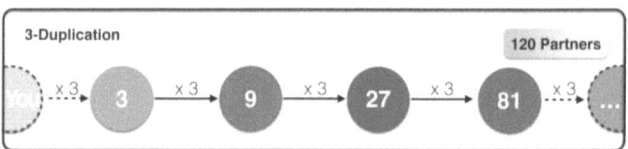

Now you explain to the '**new partners'** how you have recommended the marketing concept to your first **t h r e e** **'serious partners',** and your team grows by 27 people. A further duplication results in 81 '**new partners'**. If you now sum it up, you have a team of 120 reliable people. The size of your **team** has **increased by the factor eight**!

Comparison of the numerical series
of the 2-Duplication and the 3-Duplication

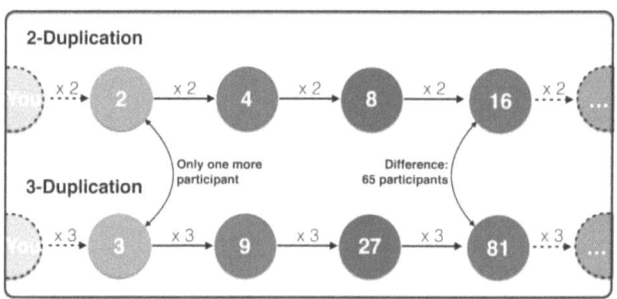

What happened now? Please notice the difference between 81 and 16 participants! You have 65 '**new partners'** more in your team!

Can you see **the difference**?

You have explained your concept to **only o n e additional person** per month successfully. From that point onwards, this procedure is transferred to all the other people involved.

Let us assume that we increase the concept **to four** 'serious partners':

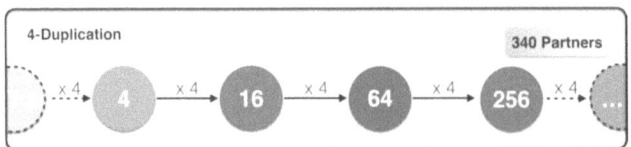

Now, you and every 'new serious partner' supports **four other 'serious partners'**. You therefore help four '**new** partners' and teach them properly, so that each of them is able to recommend and support **four** '**serious partners'** as well: This leads to 16 new partners. You now teach those 16 people how to recommend and support four '**serious** partners' as well, so that your network grows to 64 '**new** partners'. In the following month, your network will grow to a size of 340 people.

Compared to the 1-Duplication, the size of your **team has increased by the factor 22!**

And what happened now? Please notice the huge difference between 256 and 16 participants! You now have 240 '**new partners'** more in your team! Can you see **the difference**?

Comparison of the numerical series
of the 2-Duplication and the 4-Duplication

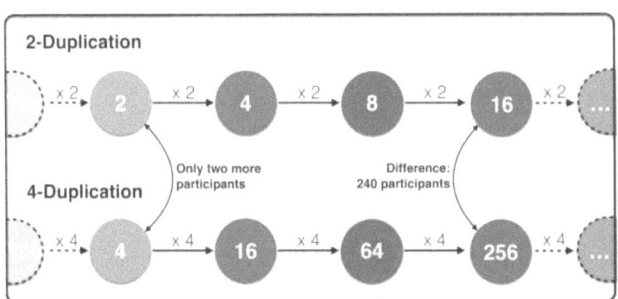

Can you see the **huge difference**?

You **only** taught your concept to **t w o additional people** per month and you transfer this procedure to all following people!

Let us assume that we now increase the concept to **f i v e 'serious partners'** per month:

Numerical series of the 5-Duplication

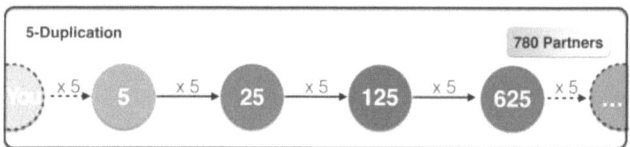

You and every member of your team now support **five 'serious partners'**. Your Referral Marketing business grows to 780 people in just four months.

Comparison of the numerical series
of the 2-Duplication and the 5-Duplication

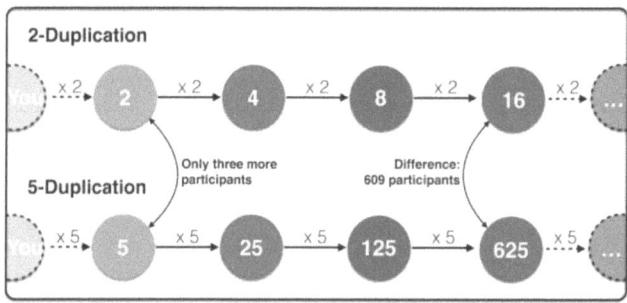

What happened? You can see the difference between 625 and 16 participants, which means you now have 609 '**new** partners' more in your team!

Can you see the **exorbitant difference**?

You and your team members recommended the Referral Marketing concept to **only   t h r e e additional people** per month and supported them. 780 people have been taught successfully, which is a fully transferable procedure. The size of your **team has increased by the factor 52!**

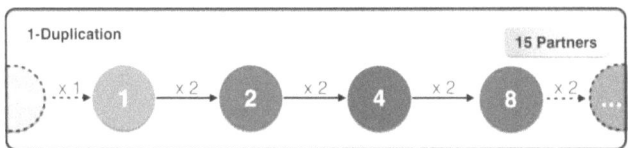

Increase of the number of partners by the **factor 2** compared to the 1-Duplication

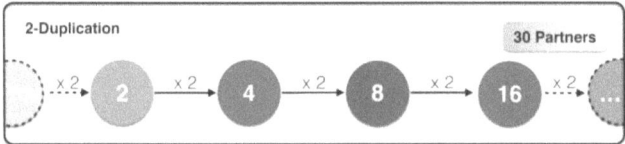

Increase of the number of partners by the **factor 8** compared to the 1-Duplication

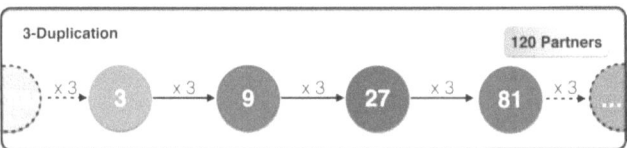

Increase of the number of partners by the **factor 22** compared to the 1-Duplication

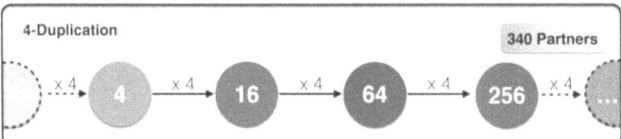

Increase of the number of partners by the **factor 52** compared to the 1-Duplication

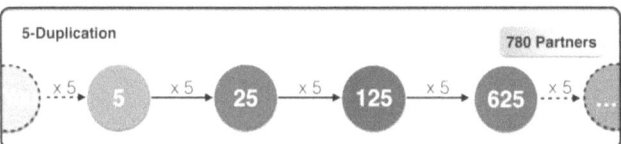

People usually can imagine supporting two, three, four or five serious partners. However, they have no apprehension of the potentiation of 16-, 81-, 256- or 625-partners.

Let us assume that you would like to support **five** '**serious partners**' to establish their business. You might not meet those partners immediately, but you may introduce 20, 40 or 60 people to the concept of Referral Marketing.

This book supports you in quickly finding the 'serious partners'
and leading those who decided to be serious to success faster.
Eike Clausius

Already by using the 5-Duplication consequently, you should have 780 'serious partners' in your network.

Now you certainly ask yourself: Did anyone buy or sell any goods to anyone by now?   – NO –

If we expect that each of your 780 '**serious** partners' buys goods for the personal use only, a huge turnover is generated[7].

Imagine now that you gain ten '**customers**' with each '**serious** partner'. This would lead to 7.800 '**customers**' next to your 780 '**serious** partners' – meaning 8.580 people who use your concept! This is a highly profitable business with only 5 '**serious partners**' and ten '**customers**' or product users per partner.

Many people do a bit!

Remember: You are only working together with 5 people directly – this is manageable. If there are more than 7 people ('the magical number of seven'), you would start building a hierarchy to limit the communication effort as it is the case in every ordinary company.

---

[7] On your journey to the '**serious** partners' you will also meet people who are interested in the goods only, or people who do not want to do anything.

You shall work with no more than 6 people directly,
otherwise you might disappoint your partners.
Eike Clausius

Notes

How do people generate their income generally and how can they do so in the Referral Marketing business? Characterising three different groups can describe this aspect easily:

1. *Group: This group of people belongs to the **hunters, gatherers and traders** – they gather working hours and exchange them for money.*

2. *Group: They live according to the '**law of sowing and harvesting'**: They always sow in spring and they harvest in autumn. We can only harvest what we have sown – if we sow grain we will harvest grain! One would not expect to harvest something that has not been sown before.*

3. *Group: Those people **plant trees**. The construction of a successful and big network as it is described in the previous chapters can be illustrated by fruitful trees.*

In the case of Referral Marketing we speak about the third group. We build the foundation for a tree. First, we will look for…

1. *soil that is suitable for our **foundation**. We dig the first holes and make sure that we have enough **water** for watering.*

2. *We then plant the first **saplings**, which will turn into*

3. ***small trees** – without big revenues for the moment. Those will become*

4. ***medium-sized trees**, where first revenues can be seen. They further grow to become*

5. ***big trees** that already make good revenues and finally become*

6. ***magnificent trees** with very good and stable revenues.*

43

For being successful, it is therefore very important to invest some time in finding promising soil. The quality of this foundation depends on your personal input: Is the soil of a proper quality or is it necessary to water and fertilise it? At this particular point, it is very important to carefully weigh the costs and benefits. Sometimes it makes sense to move on to find better and more suitable soil. The depth and constancy of this foundation are indicators for the height your trees might reach. When your trees bear fruits regularly, this can be called a **passive income**.

Every spring an apple tree shows its blooms and bears many apples in autumn. This visualises the monthly **commission payments** of a company that spreads its goods via Referral Marketing. Planting trees generates passive income. Those trees need to be watered, fertilised, cared for and sometimes trimmed so that they stay healthy. Whenever you plant trees, you should give them the time to grow instead of pulling at the saplings and hoping that this would fasten their growth.

We should take care of the trees, maintain them and wait for the time when they bear apples. Every apple contains seeds that could mean a new existence: When these seeds fall on fruitful soil, the number of trees will increase. This is real passive income – the independent construction of new existences (Steiner, 2015, S. 18f.). You must recognise the value of 'apples'! You can count the pips in an apple, but never the apples in a pip! (Steiner, 2014, S. 117)!

„The richest people in the world look for and build NETWORKS.
Everyone else looks for work."
Robert Kiyosaki

Earnings-related comparison of distribution channels

In order to recognise the advantages of Referral Marketing compared to other distribution channels, two aspects should be highlighted: In Referral Marketing you should work

1. *systematically and*
2. *with a certain system!*

It is important to work with a successful system. At the beginning
of your activities in the Referral Marketing business lots of things
will work 'on call' and without a system – as it is the case in a
small enterprise. With a growing number of people, however, it
becomes very important to systematise your actions and to make
them comprehensible for your partners. The underlying principles need to be implemented consistently.

The compensation of recommendations through the company
can be visualised in a structured **compensation plan**. You should
always work with a company that allows commissions on many
(deep) levels. This enables you to be in need of no more than five
people who are directly connected with you and who truly want
to **do** something. These people can be called 'Firstliners' (your
partners on the first, direct level). You can cooperate with them
and duplicate your system into further, deeper levels.

The following section will introduce you to the financial effects
related to the depth of your network in
(a) direct sales,
(b) a Referral Marketing concept with limited levels and
(c) a Referral Marketing concept with unlimited levels.

The difference between a commission of 30% up to the 5th level (6% per level), and a commission of 'only' 5% per level, but up to the 6th level, is demonstrated on the basis of the 5-Duplication below. This small difference of only 1 additional level and 1% less participation in sales leads to a truly impressive end result!

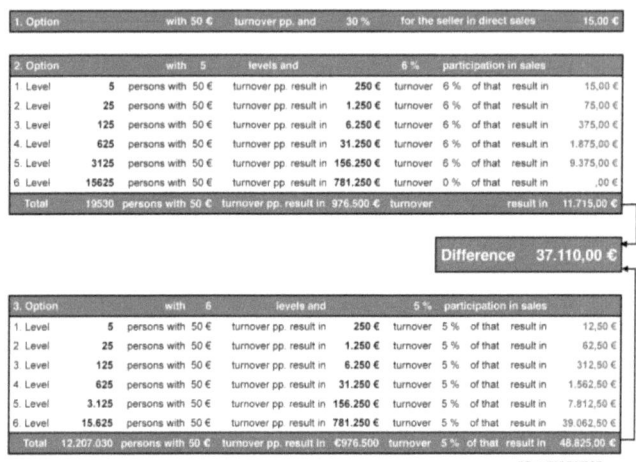

Comparison of the commissions of different distribution channels using the example of the 5-Duplication

pp. = per person

The table highlights the advantages of Referral Marketing concepts without limited levels compared to direct sales and a Referral Marketing concept with limited levels:

The first option introduces traditional direct sales. A seller receives a commission of 30% on his turnover of 50€. The more partners he has, the better is his income. It is, however, limited by the (life-)time he invests in his business.

The second option assumes that we have a 5-Duplication with a turnover of 50,00€ per participant and a commission of 30% as well. This corresponds to a typical compensation plan in Network Marketing. 30% of commissions are distributed over five levels with 6%. According to the table and a turnover of 50,00€ per participant this would result in a payment of 9.375,00€.

The third option assumes that we have a Referral Marketing concept with unlimited levels. To make it easier, only six of them are presented in the table. The commission of 30% is distributed over six levels with 5%. The payment at level five is 'only' 7.812,50€ in this case, but if we look at level six we already have 39.062,50€. The difference to the second option is therefore 29.667,50€. Every following level would increase this sum and lead to even more impressive commissions. Already ten levels with commissions of only 3% would be massive.

The following figure underlines the relation between number of levels and growth of commission payments. A huge growth of the monthly income is possible – especially in Referral Marketing! A system with more than five levels is therefore much more profitable than a system that is limited by its depth. We can see an exponential growth of commissions the deeper the system can be duplicated. It is also worth noticing that different Referral Marketing concepts have different commissions at the very deep levels.

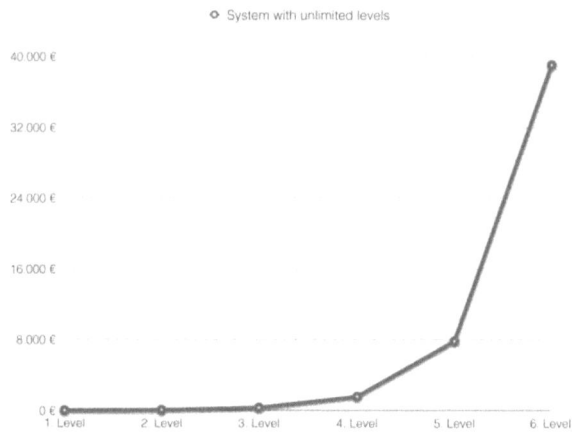

To make systems like that work, however, it is necessary to follow certain rules: **Freedom works best where clear rules are defined!**

*"It is not the strongest of the species that survives,
nor the most intelligent,
but the one most responsive to change."*
Charles Darwin

Functioning of Referral Marketing

The basics – Every beginning is hard?

Based on the above-presented financial aspects, Referral Marketing is an interesting option for everyone: Entrepreneurs and entrepreneurial thinkers, specialists and managers, employees, workers, women and men, especially single mothers (and fathers), couples, seniors, pensioners and everyone who is seriously looking for a Job (Andes, 2. Aufl., 2005, S. 24f.).

Professional sellers often fail in the Referral Marketing business (Failla, 2002, S. 17f.), because they want to apply their own 'proven' approaches. "After all, they are the experts" (Failla, 2002, S. 17). However, these 'selling-orientated' approaches cannot be transferred to other people – they are not duplicatable. One does not sell something in the Referral Marketing business; one introduces people to a simple, systematic approach and supports them in building a big and successful network. Teaching and training enables us to reproduce an existing and well-operating concept (Duplication). Sellers can become successful in the Referral Marketing business too, but they need to be open-minded to learn something new.

A selling-orientated approach leads to the issue that is illustrated by the following example: If a selling-orientated advisor (person 1) supports another selling orientated advisor (person 2) and advisor 1 quits before he was able to show advisor 2 that Referral Marketing can be very successful, advisor 2 will also quit. The result will not be a network, but only a huge number of individuals!

The limitation of a selling-orientated Referral Marketing business

49

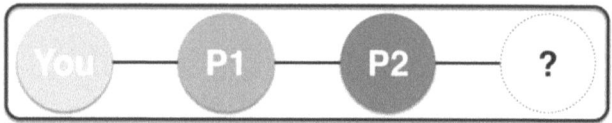

Because selling-orientated networks are hard to reproduce, the **principle of successful Referral Marketing** should be the following:

> *In the Referral Marketing business, a successful Duplication*
> *m u s t contain at least three levels in depth.*
> **Eike Clausius**

You can assume that you need to present your Referral Marketing concept to at least three **people with serious interest** in building a business. You should furthermore inform them that

1. *they can work flexible hours!*
2. *the appreciation of their work is reflected in financial acknowledgement as well as additional bonuses. That means their income can be developed according to their personal situation and ideas!*
3. *they can decide on their own whether they want to work alone or look for like-minded people to cooperate with!*
4. *they can develop a team with the people they appreciate and they can help their friends to explore their potential and to show them a new perspective in life!*
5. *they can start a career regardless of their age, sex or skin colour!*
6. *they have the opportunity to develop a business with no regional borders from their home!*
7. *they can gain courage, hope and confidence through permanent contact with positive people!*
8. *they can improve on a personal level with top-speakers at affordable seminars!*

9. *they increase the height of their pensions without the need of any deposits!*
10. *they can create financial security for their families independently from the statutory pension!*
11. *they can stay abroad as part of their new job and deduct those expenses from their taxes!*
12. *they can pass on their business to the next generation!*

As already mentioned, a **successful Duplication** needs to contain at least three levels in depth. You may show your partners how they can establish their business systematically together with you.

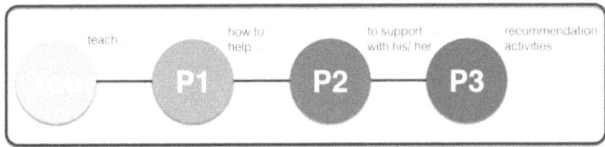

Minimum duplication of three levels in depth
of a successful Referral Marketing

A **Minimum-Duplication-Rule** could be described as follows

You teach Person 1
how to help Person 2
to support the recommendation activities of Person 3.
Eike Clausius

In doing so, it is very important to understand that **YOU** help **Person 1** to establish the business. **Person 1** does not work for **you**, but **YOU** work for **Person 1**! Person 1 should bear in mind that it is **you** who supports establishing his/her (**Person 1's**) business. **You** and **Person 1** are working together! This is a dramatic contrast to the economic structures we know, where people would work for you to earn money.

Person 1 needs to have a serious interest in establishing a business. **YOU** train **Person 1** and help him/her to develop a network together with **Person 2**. In cooperation with **Person 3** you might enlarge this network.

Only this approach leads to success: YOU support Person 1. If you stop, Person 1 will stop as well, because he or she does not know what to do. You should teach Person 1 and help him/her actively to support Person 2. This is the first step of your Duplication. If Person 1 does not learn to support Person 2 your network can never develop. This means that you may teach Person 1 how to help Person 2 to support the recommendation activities of Person 3.

If that has worked out, Person 2 can – with the support from Person 1 – recommend Person 3. Only this gives you a group that is three levels deep. It is only now that you can expect your network to continue working properly. The further transfer of your approach functions without your constant supervision. **That means that your first aim for successful Referral Marketing must be the development of a relationship network of three levels in depth!**

In the case of such relationship networks you know Person 3 via the relationships of Person 1 und Person 2. Building relationships means to establish emotional ties and to recognise peoples' uniqueness in a patient manner. (Saint-Exupéry, 1998, S. 69).

The following figures show the procedural development of your network via a depth of three or more levels. This small section aims to explain how to visualise this development in the different version of the book – the printed version and the e-book.

Printed version:

Put the book face down on a table and use it like a **flip book**[8] by flipping the pages with your thumb. You will see the process of a successful 1-Duplication with a depth of three levels.

E-book version:

To visualise the process of a successful 1-Duplication, tap or wipe twice as fast as you wish to turn the pages.

---

[8] A flip book is a book with a series of pictures that vary gradually from one page to the next, so that when the pages are turned rapidly, the pictures appear to animate by simulating motion or some other change.

Minimum duplication of three levels in depth
of a successful Referral Marketing:
- showing the process of recommending, supporting,
training and promoting - 1. Level

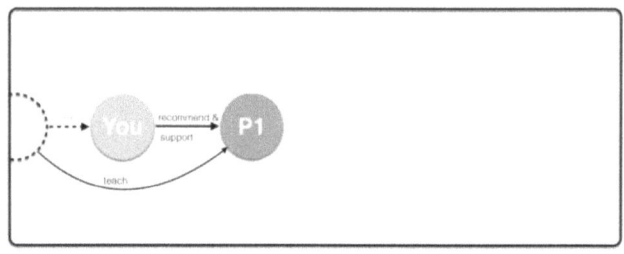

Notes

Minimum duplication of three levels in depth
of a successful Referral Marketing:
- showing the process of recommending, supporting,
training and promoting - 2. Level

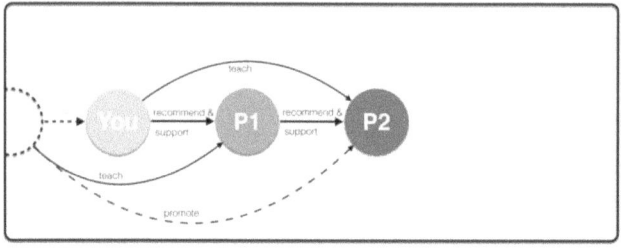

Notes

Minimum duplication of three levels in depth
of a successful Referral Marketing:
- showing the process of recommending, supporting,
training and promoting - 3. Level

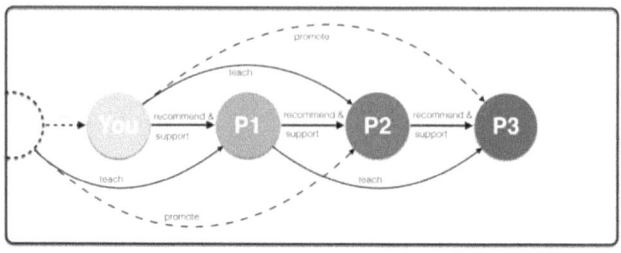

Notes

Minimum duplication of three levels in depth
of a successful Referral Marketing:
- showing the process of recommending, supporting,
training and promoting – continuous levels

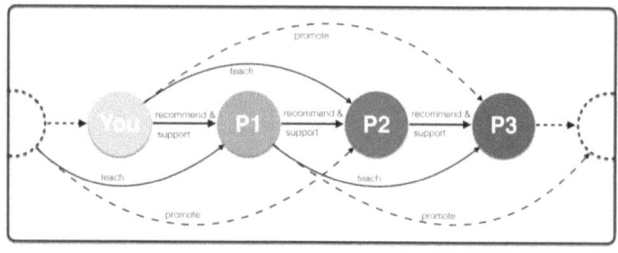

Meet up with your new partner (Person 1) and expect him/her to bring a new person (Person 2) along. When Person 1 and Person 2 meet each other, you should make sure that you attend this meeting as well. Person 1 and Person 2 know each other and you know Person 1. This leads to an immediate relationship of trust between you and Person 2 – this is **'the power of the Third Person'** for Person 1. For Person 2, you are 'the third Person' who guides him/her competently through the Referral Marketing concept. You are the competent partner who helps and supports Person 1 to establish the network with Person 2 and Person 3.

Related to the tree-metaphor, YOU could, for example, be a strong branch or the trunk, while Person 1 is a branch and Person 2 is a twig. Person 1 might be a twig as well; the only thing that matters is that YOU are at least a strong branch. You might want to invite another strong branch or trunk to the meeting, if YOU are not at this stage yet.

Now, the question is how burning enthusiasm arises and how it might be transferred to incite others! Only if many people with different, but focused motivations are coming together: One twig cannot form a (bon)fire. A twig and a branch might ignite a small flame. A twig, a branch and a strong branch will form a small fire. But only if more trunks, branches and twigs come together, the (bon)fire will truly blaze.

A meeting becomes truly 'enlightening' when you meet Person 2 together with Person 1, and Person 3 comes along with one more person. Then the five of you sit all together and a strong branch or trunk presents the Referral Marketing business.

The 'power of the Third Person' enables Person 1 to relax while you teach Person 2 the Referral Marketing business.

The ideal case would be that other people beside Person 3 attend. Then YOU support Person 3, who directly witnesses the training process of Person 2. Furthermore, one can see how the concept of Referral Marketing works: It works with the process of building a relationship network of people who support, value and train each other. It is about a personal and a business relationship and about cooperation. Competition in either business or personal aspects is counterproductive.

Only those who work continuously with a well-functioning system and the aim to establish a network with three levels in depth will be successful in the Referral Marketing business.

The Petrol Station Example illustrates how you can build a profitable (relationship-)network with Referral Marketing:

Example of a Really Magnificent Petrol Station (RMP)

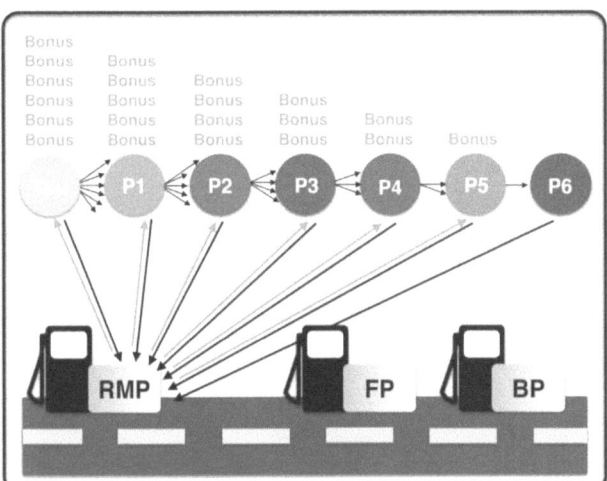

Let us assume that there are 3 petrol stations in your city. The first one is a **B**rand-Name **P**etrol Station (**BP**), the second one is a **F**ree **P**etrol Station (**FP**) and the third one is a **R**eally **M**agnificent **P**etrol Station (**RMP**). At the Brand-Name and Free Petrol Stations you get the usual service with everything you would expect. At the **R**eally **M**agnificent **P**etrol Station you can just refuel. There is no petrol pump attendant and no other service, but you can drive 20-30% further with the **special petrol** they sell. Furthermore, the customer gets a **loyalty card** that allows him to access further benefits after he has refuelled.

This petrol station offers another **special opportunity** with its loyalty card: The station saves expenses because it has no staff, rent or lease but offers fuel for the same price as other petrol stations. The resulting savings can be disbursed to those customers who recommend the RM-Petrol Station. The high savings that are not spent for staff, rent or lease can therefore be used as a **bonus** for the customers who recommend the petrol station. Depending on the amount of money that persons 1 to 5 (or others) spend at the **R**eally **M**agnificent **P**etrol Station, different bonuses will appear in the recommending members' billing.

Now let us briefly look at an important question: Who is selling the fuel in this example? The **R**eally **M**agnificent **P**etrol Station or you? ...

Correct: **R**eally **M**agnificent **P**etrol Station!
This **petrol station** has decided to sell its goods using Referral Marketing!

You only recommend while the **R**eally **M**agnificent **P**etrol Station carries out the selling process! **You sell nothing, you solely recommend,** share your passion and experience about the **R**eally **M**agnificent **P**etrol Station's great fuel.

One can raise the question as to which **kinds of goods** are suitable for the Referral Marketing business.
The goods should:
1. be consumer products with a personal benefit,
2. be storable in the medium-term (1 year),
3. be innovative,
4. be divisible in any way and
5. belong to a future-orientated industry or a future-oriented market with great potential for growth,
6. not be bound to licences or annual fees,
7. be available directly from the producer.

If those criteria are fulfilled you can assume that the Referral Marketing company you are looking at is a successful and properly tested business.

The following numerical examples indicate that this duplicating and multiplying approach leads to great financial advantages in Referral Marketing.

Let us now have a look at some specific figures. The following table basically introduces the possibilities of multiplication within a network that can lead you to a '**SECOND INCOME**'. The starting point is that you teach the concept to only one person per month (1-Duplication). The possible development of your referral network is visualised for a time scale of only half a year.

To achieve this, it is important to mention the basic functioning of the Referral Marketing business that has been introduced in the previous chapter *'The basics – Every beginning is hard?'*.

Numerical example of a monthly 1-Duplication

Duplication rate	You recommend in the 1. Monat	You recommend in the 2. Monat	You recommend in the 3. Monat	You recommend in the 4. Monat	You recommend in the 5. Monat	You recommend in the 6. Monat
	1 Persons	1 Persons	1 Persons	1 Persons	1 Persons	1 Persons
1. Level	1	2	3	4	5	6
2. Level		1	3	6	10	15
3. Level			1	4	10	20
4. Level				1	5	15
5. Level					1	6
6. Level						1
Total:	**1**	**3**	**7**	**15**	**31**	**63**
average Personal Volume (PV)						
40	40	120	280	600	1.240	2.520
50	50	150	350	750	1.550	3.150
60	60	180	420	900	1.860	3.780
70	70	210	490	1.050	2.170	4.410
80	80	240	560	1.200	2.480	5.040
100	100	300	700	1.500	3.100	6.300

500 PV	Tree	(around 100 - 250 €)	**6.000 PV**	Medium sized tree	(around 1.000 - 2.000 €)
1.500 PV	Sapling	(around 250 - 500 €)	**9.000 PV**	Big tree	(around 2.000 - 2.500 €)
3.000 PV	Small tree	(around 500 - 1.000 €)	**15.000 PV**	Magnificent tree	(more than 2.500 € plus)

Let us briefly have a look at the important terms to make this table fully understandable:

The **Duplication-Quota** specifies how many people you support in a certain period of time. In the case of the table above, it is about only one person per month. That is also where the name of the table comes from – the monthly 1-Duplication. Besides, different so-called 'Personal Volumes' (PV) are listed. You can imagine those to be something like loyalty points that you can gather by using your **loyalty card** at the **R**eally-**M**agnificent-**P**etrol-**S**tation. These points are a measure for the generated turnover and build the commissions you should receive related to the referral network. The sum of all points in your network is a direct indicator for your additional monthly income. The higher your Personal Volume, the more magnificent your tree and the bigger your monthly bonuses.

The relation between Personal Volume and the possible bonuses is described in the lower part of the table. Therefore, the tree-metaphor is reconsidered:

Let us assume that you 'refuel' for 100 Points per month. They will get your recommendation and follow your example.

During the first month you recommend one person to do the same as you do. You also teach this person to recommend the **R**eally-**M**agnificent-**P**etrol-**S**tation to another person in the following month. You should always bear the fundamental principles in mind. You may support others on their way with the referral network. By applying this principle in the following months, the other people in your network will follow your example (doing what you do) and you reach a Personal Volume of 6.300 points after no more than half a year.

If you 'refuel' for less than 100 points and your partners do the same, you will gain a lower monthly Personal Volume. A Personal Volume of 40 points of all participants on average results in a total Personal Volume of 2.520 points and a Personal Volume of 80 points of all participants on average results in a total Personal Volume of 5.040 points.

A low rate of 'refuelling' therefore impacts the total Personal Volume as well as your bonuses.

According to the numerical example of a monthly 1-Duplication as presented above, your network would double every month (in terms of people involved), and already after half a year you would have gained 63 partners. That would give you – depending on the specific Referral Marketing company – an additional monthly income of 1.000€ up to 2.000€.

If you increase the **Duplication-Quota** and recommend your concept to more than one person, even more impressive perspectives of growth are imaginable, but only if the people in your network cooperate under consideration of the precisely described principles of success you taught them. Remember that your partners will only do what you do!

The following figure compares the exponential growth of the **Single-Duplication** (1-Duplication), the **Double-Duplication** (2-Duplication) and the 3-Duplication. The solid line visualises the growth of your network in the case of the 1-Duplication. The dotted line shows a 2-Duplication and the dashed line shows that tripling your efforts will also triple the size of your network and your Personal Volume.

This refines that your efforts are adequately compensated in the Referral Marketing business. The more you recommend, the more your Personal Volume and therefore your **'SECOND IN-COME'** grows.

Comparison of exponential growth of a
1-Duplication, 2-Duplication and 3-Duplication

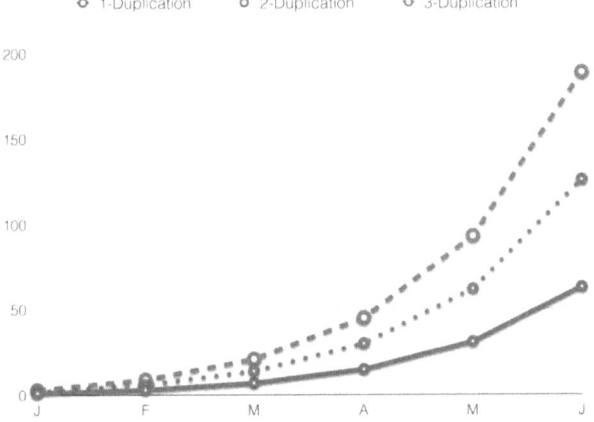

⦾ 1-Duplication   ⦾ 2-Duplication   ⦾ 3-Duplication

A qualitative view on Referral Marketing

The generation of income in Referral Marketing –
The truck metaphor

Let us assume that you have been working in the Referral Marketing business for a while now and that you have some first people who are interested in your network. Now, it is time to take care of those interested people who want to make progress in the Referral Marketing business together with you.

After you have told all interested people how easily and systematically the Referral Marketing business operates, you can choose your 'truck' and already stand at the '**warehouse**' when it is parking at the ramp of your hall. Whenever a truck drives to the ramp of your warehouse, you can make a profit out of its load.

The following figure visualises the three trucks.

Example of a warehouse with three trucks

Related to the petrol station example we want to analyse an **'Empty Truck'**, a **'Silver Truck'** and a **'Gold Truck'**. These different trucks should represent the different kinds of the interested people in your network (Failla, 2002) (Failla, Die 45-Sekunden Präsentation, die ihr Leben verändern wird, 2008).

You surely have an interest in leading many trucks that are loaded with gold to the ramp of your warehouse. So, you will lead as many Gold Trucks as possible to your ramp.

However, many people – probably because of social engagement or in order to give someone a new perspective – try to lead the empty trucks to their ramp.

The **'Gold Truck'** represents the selling-orientated advisor or the professional seller. They do not need any help, because they 'know how it works'. If they are open-minded and willing to learn, they will understand the importance of trying to establish deep levels rather than wide sales structures in Referral Marketing very quickly.

For Referral Marketing we can say:

The depth of the network beats
the width of the network.
Eike Clausius

The **'Empty Truck'** represents the people who have been in your network for months, but they permanently need to be convinced that Referral Marketing works. Their attitude is pessimistic – the glass is half empty rather than half full. Negative comments of other people or the media discourage them very quickly.

'Silver Trucks' are all new partners: It depends on the way you treat and, at best, support the truck drivers whether they will become Gold Trucks or Empty Trucks.

Our previous example of the 5-Duplication (see: Comparison of the commissions of different distribution channels) generally is about the '**Gold Trucks**'. In other words, it is about those partners who really want to **do** something: The bigger the number of 'Silver Trucks' that want to become 'Gold Trucks' in your fleet, the lower the number of people you need to contact directly to gain five **serious partners**.

Let us briefly have a look at the characteristics of those **serious partners** or **'Gold Trucks'**:

1. *Curious and anxious to learn – the new partners call you frequently because they are looking for answers to their numerous questions.*
2. *Support – the new partners are anxious to present their interested persons and to inform them about the possibilities of Referral Marketing.*
3. *Enthusiasm – the new partners are totally enthusiastic about the Referral Marketing business, because they know and understand that it works.*
4. *Commitment – the new partners are willing to commit to using the goods of your company, and they use every free minute to learn more about them and the business.*
5. *Goal-Orientation – the new partners have goals, they know why they are doing something and they are keen to do something. They note down their goals to see them clearly, in case they are losing sight of their objectives.*
6. *List of Names – the new partners have a List of Names with people they know. They can expand this list whenever possible.*
7. *Joy of the Community – the new partners feel real pleasure in sharing their business and private time together with the whole community.*
8. *Positive – the new partners will rather say 'yes' than 'no' to everything that is new. This 'positive energy' helps them attract new people.*

That **list of characteristics to recognise 'Gold Trucks'** could be continued endlessly. The only difference between a '**Silver Truck**' and a '**Gold Truck**' is their current understanding and their seriousness: **The 'Gold Truck' is doing business seriously and intelligently.**

Notes

In the following, some further figures will be used to understand the process of Duplication and the potential of the participants even better. Those are based on the 'tree-metaphor': The participants build a widely branching network. Those branches have the ability and the potential to grow even further.

A view on the monthly growth of participants in Referral Marketing will therefore be given, and the development of the different levels will be introduced.

Manual for using the following figures

Printed version:

Put the book face down on a table and use it like a **flip book**[9] by flipping the pages with your thumb. You will see the exponential growth of your group in the case of the 1-Duplication.

E-book version:

To visualise the exponential growth of your network in the case of the 1-Duplication, tap or wipe twice as fast as you wish to turn the pages. This will show the potential exponential growth of your network.

---

[9] A flip book is a book with a series of pictures that vary gradually from one page to the next, so that when the pages are turned rapidly, the pictures appear to animate by simulating motion or some other change.

The following figure is based on the assumption that you integrate **only one new serious partner** (business partner) in the first month:

Network building – 1st month in Referral Marketing
1-Duplication

You share your business with the first **serious partner** and you have explained the basic concept. He is interested and has understood the basic **principle of successful Referral Marketing**. He wants to establish his own Referral Marketing business with your help and he wants to grow. That means, your business partner will follow your example in the following months – he/she will also give someone the opportunity to shape his/her own life and to start with Referral Marketing. You work together on building and expanding your network. This leads to the following structure in the second month:

Network building – 2nd month in Referral Marketing
1-Duplication

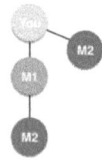

You as well as your first business partner, give another person the chance to set up a new existence – with the support from both of you. You work together with them. All of you follow the basic concept, because everyone understands the concept and puts it into practice.

That means that each of the new participants you have introduced will find another business partner in the third month. This is the point where you can see the successful 1-Duplication with three levels in depth that has already been presented in the previous section (Functioning of Referral Marketing).

You train your first serious partner (Person 1) how he can support the recommendation activities of his first serious partner (Person2) to support the recommendation activities of the following partner (Person 3). (look also: Minimum duplication of three levels in depth)

Network building – 3rd month in Referral Marketing
1-Duplication

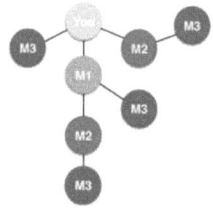

Ideally, you have built your first stable line with three serious partners and you can now focus on enhancing its strength.

Under the premise that the concept has been properly communicated and understood, all of the participants will offer the possibilities of Referral Marketing to one more person in the following month.

Network building – 3rd month in Referral Marketing
1-Duplication with the first 'stable line'

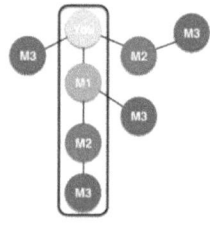

In the fourth month it becomes clear for the first time that the system multiplies and grows faster and faster in the course of time – it grows disproportionally.

Therefore, three new stable 1-Duplications with three levels are created, two of which start from your first serious partner and another one from your second serious partner in the first level.

At the same time, the first **1-Duplication** with three levels in depth where you are not involved anymore is created (M1 to M4). This one has been built from your first serious partner who takes over your role. You might, however, still provide assistance and support whenever needed.

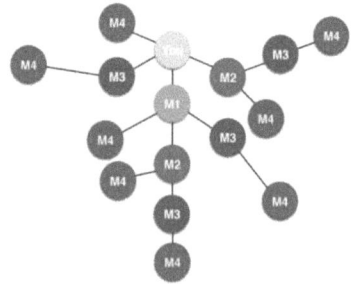

In the fifth month, the effect of multiplication becomes even clearer. Sixteen new serious partners join your Referral Marketing network. Furthermore, six new 1-Duplications with three levels are created. This increases the stability and independence of your system significantly.

In total, you now have 32 people and 10 direct 1-Duplications with three levels (that involve you directly) in your network.

86

In the sixth month – which is the last month we will analyse for this example – your Referral Marketing network has grown to 64 people. Of course, this only works under the premise that the functionality of the concept has been communicated properly and applied consistently.

Now it also becomes clear why it is that important to systematise the approaches and to make them understandable for all parties involved. Only **simplicity**, **systematisation** and **transparency** make Referral Marketing successful. Every change and deviation creates non-duplicatable networks that stop growing very quickly. A strong network cannot be built when the levels change frequently.

The Referral Marketing concept needs to stay clear, simple, systematic and duplicatable. At the same time, however, it also needs to take into account personal and individual aspects, but without allowing changes at the most fundamental level of the concept.

Network building – 6th month in Referral Marketing
1-Duplication

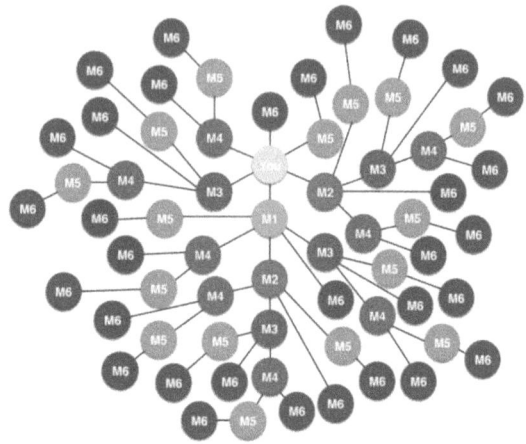

These figures have clearly shown the potential of the duplication of a simple basic concept. The explosive nature mainly lies in the application of this basic concept in very deep levels. The system's 'width' grows automatically. Related to the **'tree-metaphor',** one could say that the crown of the tree becomes tighter, bigger and more complex. A tree that grows wide (with many ramifications in the first level) needs more personal investment than a tree that rather grows high with many branches in the crown.

It is very important to understand that a complex structure can only develop because of a simple basic concept. Only such Referral Marketing networks are understandable and duplicatable.

> *The simpler the basic concept,*
> *the more powerful the (tree-)structure.*
> *The more complex the basic concept,*
> *the more slender the (tree-)structure.*
> **Eike Clausius**

Printed version:

Put the book face down on a table and use it like a **flip book**[10] by flipping the pages with your thumb. You will see the growth of your network in the case of a 1-Duplication per level in depth.

E-book version:

To visualise the growth of your network per level in depth in the case of the 1-Duplication, tap or wipe twice as fast as you wish to turn the pages.

---

[10] A flip book is a book with a series of pictures that vary gradually from one page to the next, so that when the pages are turned rapidly, the pictures appear to animate by simulating motion or some other change.

Let us now look into the situation related to the emerging levels or the emerging depth of the system. The resulting figure shows the development of your Referral Network after just 6 months by using the **1-Duplication** (one recommendation per month).

The figure below introduces the first level after 6 months and therefore contains 6 people.

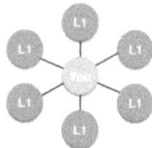

During the first six months you and your partners have built a 2nd level with 15 people. Your business partners of the 1st level have been taught how recommendations and sharing of a successful system works. This concept has been implemented consistently.

Network building – up to the 2nd level in Referral Marketing
1-Duplication

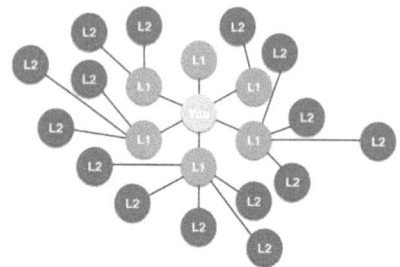

The next figure additionally shows the 3rd level and contains the first successful 1-Duplication with a depth of the three levels that have been reached in the third month.

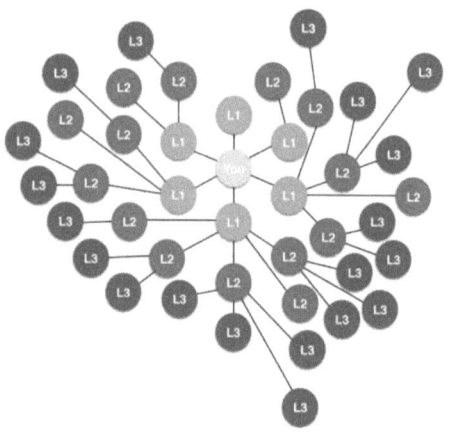

Within the demonstrated six months the network is further branched in the 4th level. This is visualised in the following figure.

Network building – up to the 4th level in Referral Marketing
1-Duplication

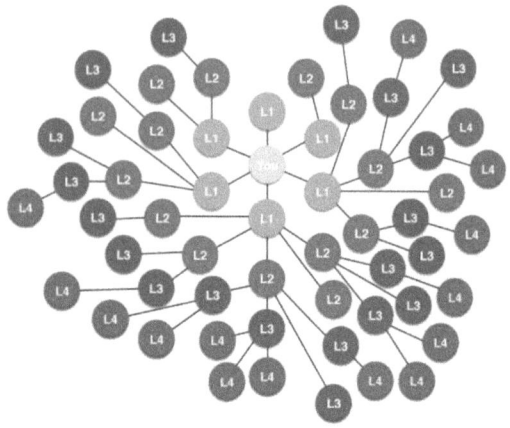

In the 6th month the network is also branched in the 5th level, which is visualised in the following figure.

Network building – up to the 5th level in Referral Marketing
1-Duplication

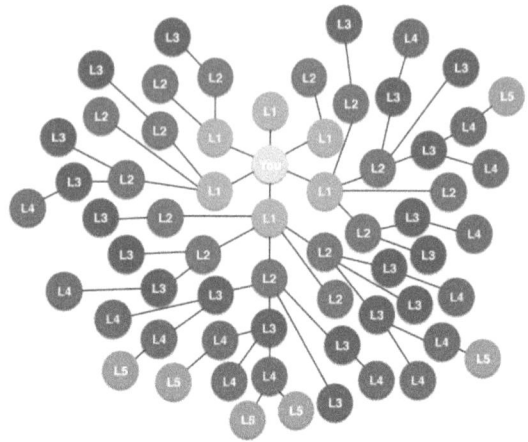

The last figure shows the complete structure of your Referral Network with all business partners and a depth of up to 6 levels in the 6th month. Remember that continuing this approach in the 7th month will lead to even more impressive results. After just one year of basic conceptual growth, you would have 4.095 people in your network.

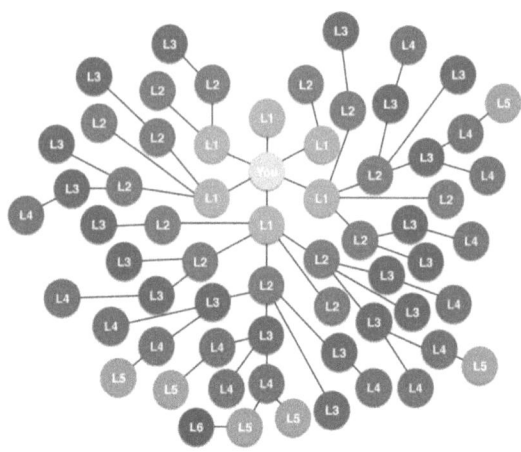

You and 63 partners:

1. *Level –   6 persons,*
2. *Level – 15 persons,*
3. *Level – 20 persons,*
4. *Level – 15 persons,*
5. *Level –   6 persons,*
6. *Level –   1 person*

In the following chapter, some numbers related to this network shall underline the possibilities of your 'SECOND INCOME'.

A quantitative view on Referral Marketing

Income opportunities after six months of 1-Duplication

The following figure shows all people and their individual levels after a successful **1-Duplication** over half a year. It is a rearrangement of the network that has been introduced in the previous chapter and it is combined with some numerical examples. The figure demonstrates the possible commissions by way of showing exemplary turnovers.

Referral Marketing: Income after 6 months
in case of the 1-Duplication

Income after 6 months in case of the 1-Duplication with 80PV / 100€

Level		PV	Commission
		80 PV	
Level 1 10%		480 PV	ca. 60,00€
Level 2 10%		1.200 PV	ca. 150,00€
Level 3 10%		1.600 PV	ca. 200,00€
		3.360 PV	ca. 410,00€
Level 4 5%		1.200 PV	75,00€
Level 5 5%		480 PV	30,00€
Level 6 5%		80 PV	5,00€
		5.120 PV	ca. 520,00€

An example of a Personal Volume (PV) of 80 PV per person and month would be equal to a turnover of 100€.
You have gained six business partners at the first level within six months. Based on the assumption that every partner – just like

103

you – buys goods for 80 PV, your total turnover would be equal to 600€ in the first level.

If we assume that you receive a commission of 10 percent, this would mean 60€. The turnover at the second and third level is also funded with 10 percent in this example[11]. This adds up to an amount of around 410€ through commissions at the first three levels.

As already mentioned, systems that are unlimited in the depth of their levels can lead to even more impressive additional incomes. It is understandable that no company can pay very high commissions down to those very deep levels. Because every person in the Referral Network buys goods directly from the producer, the costs of the commissions are included in the product price. This correlation has been shown in the figure ‚**composition of a customer price - direct sale**‘. In the case of a product price of 100€ and compared to traditional ways of distribution, 70% of the distribution costs are paid as commissions. For that reason, the example given above assumes commissions of only 5% for the third and up to the sixth level. So, a further additional income of 110€ is generated.

Your '**SECOND INCOME**' could therefore sum up to **520€ per month** after just **half a year of successful Referral Marketing** and only one successful **1-Duplication**.

What would a 'SECOND INCOME' like that mean to you from a financial point of view?

---

[11] The percentages in this case are chosen as an example and can vary depending on the individual Referral Marketing company.

Let us assume that you are interested in a '**SECOND INCOME**' of 500€. Which opportunities would you have to receive those 500€?

A **first possibility** could be working for 40 additional hours per month with an hourly wage of 12,50€ – ten hours per week.

A **second possibility** could be to place money with a bank and to receive interest – under the condition that you already have this money. With, for example, 100.000€ you would need a bank that offers an interest rate of 6 percent per annum in order to receive 500€ per month. However, in the case of a realistic **interest rate** of 0,5% (in 2016), you would need the exorbitant sum of 1.200.000€!

The following table introduces further possibilities of **capital formation** with different **investment amounts** (from 100.000€ to 1.200.000€). These will help to calculate which monthly return is possible in which case.

Capital formation by different investment amounts
and different interest rates

Consideration per month						
	Investment amount					
Interest rate	100.000 €	200.000 €	300.000 €	400.000 €	600.000 €	1.200.000 €
0,50 %	42 €	83 €	125 €	167 €	250 €	**500 €**
1,00 %	83 €	167 €	250 €	333 €	**500 €**	1.000 €
1,50 %	125 €	250 €	375 €	**500 €**	750 €	1.500 €
2,00 %	167 €	333 €	**500 €**	667 €	1.000 €	2.000 €
3,00 %	250 €	**500 €**	750 €	1.000 €	1.500 €	3.000 €
6,00 %	**500 €**	1.000 €	1.500 €	2.000 €	3.000 €	6.000 €

If you do not have such **amounts of money**, you need to work for it during the next years. Under the assumption that you set aside 'only' 1.000€ per month, you would need to save this money for 100 months – which equals approximately eight years – to get the **sum** of 100.000€. But then, it is still necessary to find a bank that gives you an **interest rate** of 6% per annum. In order to raise 1.200.000€ in the same way, you would need 100 years! (One can then question whether you would still be there to receive the payment.)

Capital formation by different investment amounts

100.000 €	sum of savings		1.200.000 €	sum of savings
1.000 €	reserve per month results in		1.000 €	reserve per month results in
100	months and therefore		1.200	months and therefore
8,33	years		100	years

A **third possibility** is the creation of an additional income through Referral Marketing. As the example underlines, for that you only need six people in six months (see: Numerical example of a monthly 1-Duplication). The **serious partners** of your Referral Marketing network can realise this monthly flow of cash. This cash flow would be a 'pension', which you never needed to pay something in for. A **Referral Marketing concept** creates the possibility to work on your business intensively for four years rather than paying money into the **statutory pension** funds for 40 years with no security of receiving any payments (dab/dpa, 2014).

4 years of Referral Marketing or
40 years of paying into the statutory pension funds?
Eike Clausius

„A judgement can be refuted, but never a prejudgement."
Marie Freifrau von Ebner-Eschenbach

Step by step to your Second Income

Reality check

At this point, you might ask yourself whether and how those numbers could become your reality.

One thing is clear: If you receive any wages or salary at the moment and you retire, your income development will look as demonstrated in the following figure.

Your salary or income will be reduced to less than 50% according to the governmentally prescribed adjustments.

Therefore, this chapter aims at describing how you could start working with Referral Marketing – step by step. This principle always functions in the same way, independently from the specific company.

It has already been pointed out that starting with Referral Marketing works without any personal and financial risk. Let us stay with our example from the previous section: At the beginning you are only using an offer and the '**special petrol**' that allows you to drive 20% - 30% further. Perhaps a friend recommended this special petrol to you. Or perhaps someone introduced you to the Referral Marketing business directly. You are a 'Referral Marketing Product User'. Whichever way brought you to Referral Marketing, by the time you see that the business model functions, your interest starts to grow.

You start to spend more time on the concept and you recommend the goods to your friends. After a while, you recognise that you can refinance your monthly 'fuel' that way. You have become a 'Referral Marketing Partner'. Your current income will be increased by the commissions of your Referral Marketing company. At this point, you have to make a decision: Do you want to continue earning money with Referral Marketing? When you decide to choose this path, you should increasingly systematise your approaches. Here, the **Minimum-Duplication-Rule** as a basis for the successful duplication plays an important role: **You** teach **Person 1** how to help **Person 2** to support the recommendation activities of **Person 3**. Build your network and work with those who really want to support you and who show enthusiasm. You can also trust on the help of people who already work with this concept. Step by step, your recommendation activities grow into a 'Part-time Referral Marketing partnership'.

The commissions will further increase your current income. When you retire, now your pension will be increased by the commissions and you create your own 'pension increase' with Referral Marketing.

If any problems with your current income appear, you now have the security of a solid financial basis that can be expanded further.

If you become more and more successful with your systematic approach, you might reach the point where the income of your Referral Marketing business – **your 'SECOND INCOME'** – exceeds your current income. At this point at the latest, you will think about the possibility that this part-time job might grow to your new 'Full-Time Referral Marketing Partnership'. Meanwhile, you constantly build up your 'SECOND INCOME' and – at the same time – a permanent pension that can benefit you after your career.

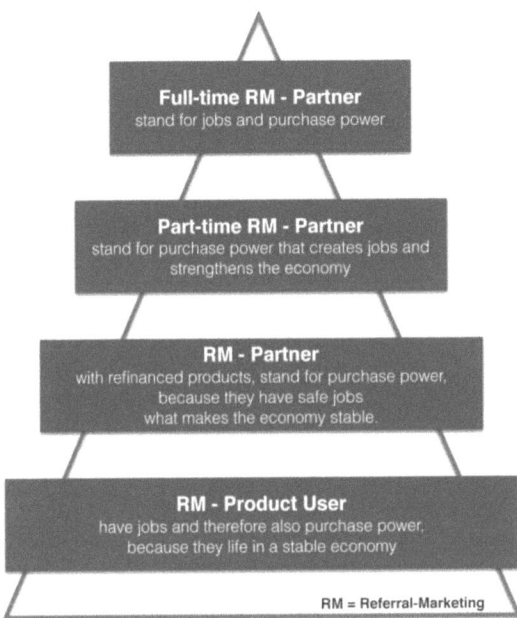

Full-time RM - Partner
stand for jobs and purchase power

Part-time RM - Partner
stand for purchase power that creates jobs and
strengthens the economy

RM - Partner
with refinanced products, stand for purchase power,
because they have safe jobs
what makes the economy stable.

RM - Product User
have jobs and therefore also purchase power,
because they life in a stable economy

RM = Referral-Marketing

Please mention what was already suggested in the previous chapter: Your partner will most probably act like you. Depending on how much time and energy you invest in this work, you will reach your goals more or less quickly. It is your decision, which paths you want to choose in the Referral Marketing business.

The above figure is a visualisation of the possible career of a successful Referral Marketer and demonstrates the outlined path with its different stages.

The 1-3-5-7-Rule

Based on experience, there is a **role of thumb** related to the progress in the Referral Marketing business. This enables you to get
an idea of the time it takes to grow from a 'Referral Marketing
Product User' to a 'Full-Time Referral Marketing Partner'.

1st Year

*In the first year you should be competent enough to establish a
profitable Referral Marketing business that you could run part-
time.*

3rd Year

*If you are running a Referral Marketing business on a part-time
basis and you recommend continuously and systemically, you
come to a point at which you could decide to make Referral
Marketing your full-time profession.*

5th Year

*After mastering Referral Marketing for five years in a continu-
ous and systematic way, you could generate a six-digit salary
and become an expert.*

7th Year

*After seven years of continuously working in the Referral Mar-
keting business, you are an expert and know the ropes of Referral Marketing.*

This should clarify that you are able to create a permanent 'SEC-
OND INCOME', a stable and additional source of earnings. When
you become an expert in the field of Referral Marketing, it is possible to do it full-time.

You will see that Referral Marketing is a learning process – learning by doing.

This learning process will lead you through the following stages:

1) *Unconscious Incompetence* - *You do not know that you don't know it. – When you have never heard of Referral Marketing, this is unconscious incompetence.*

2) **Conscious Incompetence** - *You do know that you don't know it and that you can learn it. – When you are aware of knowing very little about Referral Marketing and that you should learn something about it, this is conscious incompetence.*

   You will be surprised how many people you meet who are not willing to learn anything new and who think that they already know everything. Until now, I have only met barbers who needed five or seven years to become real masters of their profession. It is very interesting that some people tell you they "don't need to learn Referral Marketing!" This is rarely the case. You should try to help those people to overcome this stage; otherwise they will not be successful in the Referral Marketing business. You cannot help someone who doesn't want your help. When people do not want to learn something new, you should focus on someone else.

3) **Conscious Competence** - *You do know that you know it. You learn and you are willing to learn. – You make mistakes and you learn from your mistakes. Continuous training helps all of us to become even better.*

4) **Unconscious Competence** - *You don't know that you know it. Now you have reached a stage where your skills are automatised and the way you act develops in a professional way. At this stage, you have become a professional Referral Marketer. You do and say things without really having to*

115

Please bear in mind that everyone could recognise Referral Marketing as his new profession – if he/she only wants to. You can learn those skills with the support of the **right mentors**. **If you do not believe in yourself yet, for now you can trust me, because I know what I've written.** Moreover, there are many other successful people in the Referral Marketing business who you can trust and believe.

You can learn Referral Marketing in the same way you have learned many other things before, from tying your shoes or riding a bike to driving a car or even flying an airplane. Everything is learnable.

Enjoy the freedom and the lifestyle of a Referral Marketer – give it a try and start looking for successful **mentors**. We are looking forward to meeting you!

Bibliography

Andes, W. (2. Aufl., 2005). Die Kraft von Network Marketing. Eine seriöse Vertriebsform für unternehmerisch denkende Menschen. *Schnellbach.*

Bundesverband, N. M. (Version 2.01 2005). Network Marketing - eine neue Selbstständigkeit. *Abgerufen am 10. 5. 2015 von http://mlm18.de/wp-content/uploads/2012/10/Bundesverband-Network-Marketing-und-Prof.-Dr.-Michael-M.-Zacharias-Was-ist-Network-Marketing.pdf*

Clausius, E. (1998). Betriebswirtschaftslehre I - Einführung in hierarchischen Modulen *(Bd. 1). München: Oldenbourg.*

Clausius, E. (1999). Betriebswirtschaftslehre II - Finanzierung und Investition in hierarchischen Modulen *(Bd. 2). München: Oldenbourg.*

Clausius, E. (2012). Vom Wutbürger zum Mutbürger – Wie Gedankenenergien die Gesellschaft verändern können. In T. V. Masárová, Personalmanagement in bewegten Zeiten *(S. 323-328). Plauen: M&S Verlag.*

Clausius, E. (2014). BetriebsWirtschaftsLehre - Band 1 - Einführung. *Norderstedt: BoD - Books on Demand.*

Clausius, E. (2015). Paradigmenwechsel in der Wirtschaft - von der rationalen zur emotionalen Intelligenz. *Norderstedt: BoD-Books on Demand.*

Clausius, E., & Schütz, M. (2014). Die Schattenseite des Erfolgs – Produktpiraterie im Maschinen- und Anlagenbau. *Norderstedt: BoD-Books on Demand.*

dab/dpa. (02. 12. 2014). Abrechnung des Ex-Arbeitsministers: Blüm hält die Rente nicht mehr für sicher. *Abgerufen am 08. 08. 2015 von http://www.spiegel.de/wirtschaft/soziales/norbert-bluem-haelt-rente-nicht-mehr-fuer-sicher-a-1006121.html*

Failla, D. (2002). Ihre Zukunft - Das Erfolgkonzept - Wie Sie jetzt ein zusätzliches Einkommen von 2.000,-€ und mehr von Ihrem Wohnzimmer aus aufbauen! *Fellbach: MOM Media Medien-& Verlagsges. mbH.*

Failla, D. (2008). Die 45-Sekunden Präsentation, die ihr Leben verändern wird *(2. Aufl. Ausg.). Innsbruck.*

Gallup GmbH & Financial Times Deutschland. (2014). Gallup-Studie 2014: Nur jeder siebte Arbeitnehmer ist von seinem eigenen Job wirklich begeistert.

Ihringer, U. W. (März 2014). Die neue Selbständigkeit - Warum Network Marketing boomt -. Network Press, *7(41), 48-56.*

Kiyosaki, R. (2012). Das Geschäft des 21. Jahrhunderts. *Innsbruck.*

Kiyosaki, R., Fleming, J., & Kiyosaki, K. (2012). The Business of the 21st Century. *(M. P. Ltd, Hrsg.)*

Kremer, A. J. (2000). Reich durch Beziehungen. Durch die richtigen Kontakte zum Erfolg. *Landsberg am Lech: verlag moderne industrie.*

Saint-Exupéry, A. d. (1998). Der kleine Prinz *(52. Ausg.). Karl Rauch.*

Steiner, G. (2014). From Person to Person – Earning a Stable Income from Referral Marketing *(1. Edition Ausg.). Weinstadt: Andreas Steiner e.K.*

Steiner, G. (2015). From Person to Person 2 - Insights and Stories. *Weinstadt: Andreas Steiner e.K.*

Tepperwein, K. (2005). Lebenskünstler leben leichter. *Güllesheim.*

Worre, E. (2013). GoPRo - 7 Schritte zum Network Marketing Profi. *Innsbruck: Life Success Media GmbH.*

Index

How to use the index of the e-book:
     To find the word use the blue arrow.
How to use the index of the book:
     To find the word use the number of the page.

About the author

Prof. Dr. Eike Clausius

Dr. Eike Clausius studied Economy and Industrial Chemistry in Berlin, Netherlands, Czechoslovakia and the U.S.A. He finished his study as a Dipl.-Ing. /TU at the Technical University of Berlin (TUB) in 1983.

After several years working in different kinds of industrial companies he made his PhD (Dr. rer. oec.) in 1992 at the TU Berlin in 'Controlling in Research and Development'. He is a specialist in combining economical and technical aspects in business. Since that time he supports people on their ways in Network-Marketing, Multi-Level-Marketing und Referral Marketing. As a partner of different franchise systems he signed in various kinds of companies and checked these widespread economic models of their seriority und effectiveness!

In 1994 he got a call at the University of Applied Sciences in Zwickau/Germany concerning business administration and emotional intelligence. He expended his knowledge in the field of emotional intelligence by various research projects and created meanwhile the

Emotional-**I**ntelligence-as-**K**ey-**E**lement-Method (**EIKE-Method).**

Dr. Clausius is bestselling author of numerous different scientific books, Healthy-Living- und Mental-Coach as well as personality trainer. As coach and universal trainer he led different companies to their peak performance.

With his family he lives in Berlin/ Germany.

Contact to the author for seminars and Referral Marketing support:

Email: ecl@eikeclausius.de;

Homepage: www.eikeclausius.de; www.EIKE-Methode.de;
www.the-second-income.org; www.the-second-income.de

Notes

Notes

Notes

Notes

Notes

Notes

Notes

Notes

presented by: